Four Daily Exercises

(First Set of Occasional Technics)

for

Advanced Students and Artists

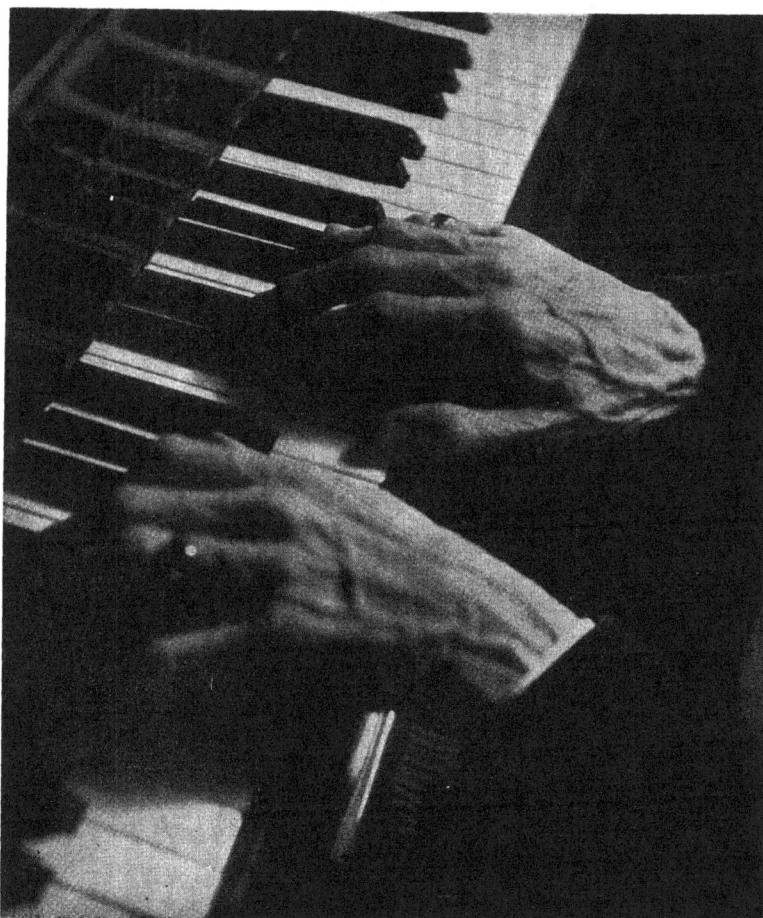

[PAUL SNYDER

By

TOBIAS MATTHAY

WINTHROP ROGERS EDITION

Sole Selling Agents:

BOOSEY & HAWKES, LTD., LONDON

Tobias Matthay

Tobias Augustus Matthay was born on 19th February 1858, in Clapham, Surrey, England. He was an English pianist, teacher and composer.

Matthay's parents originally came from northern Germany and eventually became naturalised British subjects. He studied composition at the 'Royal Academy of Music' (London) under Sir William Sterndale Bennett and Arthur Sullivan, and piano with William Dorrell and Walter Macfarren. Matthay served as a sub-professor there from 1876 to 1880, and became an assistant professor of pianoforte in 1880, before being promoted to professor in 1884.

Alongside Frederick Corder and John Blackwood McEwen (both composers and music teachers), he founded the Society of British Composers in 1905. This organisation was established with the aim of protecting the interests of British composers and to provide publication, promotion and performance opportunities. It was disbanded thirteen years later, in 1918. Matthay remained at the Royal Academy of Music until 1925, when he was forced to resign because McEwen – his former student who was then the Academy's Principal – publicly attacked his teaching.

In 1903, after over a decade of observation, analysis, and experimentation, Matthay published *The Act of Touch*, an encyclopaedic volume that influenced piano pedagogy throughout the English-speaking world. So many students were soon in quest of his insights that two years later he opened the Tobias Matthay Pianoforte School, first in Oxford Street, then in 1909 relocating to Wimpole Street, where it remained for the next thirty years. He soon became known for his teaching principles that stressed proper piano touch and analysis of arm movements. He wrote several additional books on piano technique that brought him international recognition, and in 1912 he published *Musical Interpretation*, a widely read book that analyzed the principles of effective musicianship.

Many of Matthay's pupils went on to define a school of twentieth century English pianism, including York Bowen, Myra Hess, Clifford Curzon, Moura Lympany, Eunice Norton, Lytle Powell, Irene Scharrer, Lilias Mackinnon, Guy Jonson, Vivian Langrish and Harriet Cohen. He was also the teacher of Canadian pianist Harry Dean, English composer Arnold Bax and English conductor Ernest Read.

In his private life, Matthay married Jessie (née Kennedy) in 1893, the sister of Marjory Kennedy-Fraser (the Scottish singer, composer and arranger). She sadly died in 1937.

Tobias Matthay died at his country home, High Marley, near Haslemere, on 15th December 1945. He was eighty-seven years old.

Winthrop Rogers Edition

Four Daily Exercises

for

Advanced Students and Artists

(First Set of Occasional Technics)

By

TOBIAS MATTHAY

PRICE **3**/- NET

PREFACE

When our dog gets up in the morning, he stretches his two front paws out as fully as possible, and then his two back legs as far as they will go. This is followed by a good (rotatory) shake, beginning at his head and finishing with his tail. After this he feels quite ready for the day's exploits—and he hasn't wasted any time in dressing rooms !

Often, we advanced players and artists also feel all the better for a good stretch and shake-up of our playing apparatus in the morning.

These Four Exercises are designed for this purpose, for advanced players and artists.

No. 1 is a fullest-extension five finger exercise, also involving side-to-side lateral movements of fingers, hand and wrist.

Nos. 2 and 3 are the most important of these four exercises. These, anyway, should be practised every day for five or ten minutes, since they ensure the waking-up of AGILITY conditions. Agility mainly depends upon absolute *accuracy* in the " aiming " of each note's production—so short as not to be wasted on the key-beds. The close repetitions demanded in these exercises are obviously impossible without such accuracy in *timing* each note ; hence these exercises *ensure* Agility.

No. 2 consists of closely repeated notes allied with fullest lateral movements of the thumb, hand and wrist.

No. 3 substitutes repetition of " double-notes " for the single notes in the preceding exercise.

No. 4 gives the " closest position " arpeggio, which again involves rapid, clean reiterations, but now between the two hands.

A few " extra " exercises are given as suggestions.

Full instructions for each exercise are offered for those who care to take the trouble to read them. Most musicians, however, overlook such helpful offers, and then proceed to lament failures and misunderstandings. " A stitch in time saves nine ! "

TOBIAS MATTHAY,

High Marley,

December 30th, 1938.

GENERAL INSTRUCTIONS

In practising these exercises bear in mind the following rules :—

1. Insist upon *perfect freedom* all through, however great the extensions. If you play stiffly you are practising badly ; and if your nervous equipment is unhappily such that it will not admit of your learning to play freely, then it will be far better for you to give up the piano, or any gymnastic pursuit, and resign yourself to being say " a butcher, a baker or candlestickmaker ! "

   The term " Stiffness " is here used in its accepted sense, *i.e.*, the muscular exertion of a limb impeded by its opposite, contrary or " antagonistic " exertion. Freedom simply implies the elimination of all such defeative exertions. Therefore, do everything perfectly freely.*

   Freedom certainly does not imply omission of the momentary exertions (sometimes quite considerable) required from hand and fingers—and even of the arm.

2. Insist upon carefully " aiming " (or timing) each individual key-descent accurately TO TONE. If you, instead, misfire the required force on to the felt pads under the keys, you can neither achieve *musical accuracy* of tone, nor any true *Agility*.† Hence, instead of trying to draw tone from the floor *via* the key-pads, these gifted ones, from the beginning, have acquired this trick of aiming their efforts accurately, each effort to its purpose—that is, never too late in key-descent.

   Such accuracy in *tone-production* applies equally whether you allow the keys to rebound for staccato, or choose to hold them down for legato.

   Therefore, always remember to perform each exercise with the closest possible key-attention—rhythmical, tonal and durational. These exercises must never be strummed through " regardless ".

3. The limit of attention with such routine-work will soon be reached, and then will be impaired that strict *bond of association* between MUSIC and TECHNIQUE which it should ever be our aim to further and strengthen.

   If follows, therefore, that such exercises must never be worked at *too long at a time*. The whole ground can easily be covered *in 10 or 15 minutes* !

4. Here, as in all brilliant passage-playing, be sure " to keep the arm off "—which means : keep it in its " floating " condition, nicely balanced by its own muscles, neither squeezed down on the keyboard nor left to rest too heavily on it. This " poised " condition is a *sine quo non* in all agility playing. If you are vague about this, raise your arms off the keyboard (a foot or so) and balance them in the air, allowing your hands to hang down limply from the wrists, then carry this free condition down to the keyboard.

5. Obey the laws of forearm rotation all along, else, after all, everything will go wrong.

6. All four of these exercises are particularly designed to promote *lateral* freedom. See to it therefore, that the side-to-side movements of the finger, hand and wrist are provided restraintlessly. The elbow, however should remain quiescent.

7. All these exercises should be practised as quickly as you can. The close repetitions during Nos. 2, 3 and 4 then *ensure* avoidance of agility-destroying " key-bedding".

8. Practise them sometimes *forte* but mostly *piano*. Occasionally try them *legato*, but mostly all through with " resilient " keys and fingers.

9. Practise either with " bent " or " flat " finger-action (the out-folding or in-folding finger) or if you prefer it, with that *half-way* action—half-way between such pushing and clinging-action. *See* page 79, " The Visible and Invisible." *Oxford University Press.*

*To prevent any quibbling, it is of course admitted that however successfully we do relax, there always remains a slight residue of tension which we cannot eliminate by force of will. This, no doubt, differs with each individual, and the actual time of day, and has a strong influence on so-called muscular talent.

†I, personally, am convinced that the explanation of those " Lightning-fingers " and " Lightning octaves " some players exhibit, largely resolves itself into a keen rhythmical talent.

CONTENTS

PAGE

PREFACE 1

GENERAL DIRECTIONS 1

FIRST DAILY EXERCISE, for fullest extensions 2

SECOND DAILY EXERCISE, for horizontal freedom 6

THIRD DAILY EXERCISE, for repetition on double notes 10

FOURTH DAILY EXERCISE, for closest position arpeggio 12

SOME EXTRA TECHNICS :

     No. 1 On fullest contraction 15

     No. 2 Sustained notes exercises 16

     No. 3 For lateral freedom of thumb, etc. 18

     No. 4 For " lightning " octaves 19

     No. 5 Interspersed double-notes 19

     No. 6 On Chopin's Study, No. 1 20

     No. 7 The old two-finger exercises 21

THE PURPOSE OF TECHNICAL EXERCISES 22

FIRST DAILY EXERCISE

FULLEST EXTENSION FIVE FINGER EXERCISE

First read the Preamble of General Instructions ; then these Special Directions. This exercise was designed for my own rather large hand as here noted ; but it must be practised with much caution, and mostly with quite " springy " touch, lightly, else harm instead of good will accrue.

Small hands should preferably use the alternate versions provided.

Never allow the extreme extensions to lead you astray into stiffness—always Freedom, Ease !

See to it that the arm is kept in its "floating" condition, neither pressed down on the keyboard, nor heavily resting upon it.

Remember, that the tone-producing impulse must be accurately timed for each sound, if agility conditions are to be fulfilled—it is always a rhythmical act, and the keys must be allowed to rebound all along.

Unlike most practice, all these exercises should usually be practised as swiftly as possible ; but sometimes also practised at a moderate speed—say at that of the *Finale* of Beethoven's Op. 26 in A flat. Most frequently, however, they should be practised at full Chopinesque speed.

Practise either " flat finger " or " bent finger " actions (folding-in, or un-folding actions) and sometimes with that " halfway " house—so useful at times—with the nail-joint moving and acting straight down.

Sometimes practise legato, but mostly with the aforesaid springy, *staccatissimo* touch.

N.B.—Never practise one exercise too long at a time.

The whole of these " Four Daily Exercises " can quite profitably be worked through in about 10 or 15 minutes.

A For Large Hands

Tempo — about that of Finale from Beethoven's Sonata in A flat. Op. 26.

Copyright 1939 by Boosey & Co. Ltd.   Printed in England   H. 15119

Or alternatively taken
in similar motion:—

etc.

Or varied by starting on
other notes— thus for
instance:—

etc.

Or:—

etc.

Or the following:—

a)

b)

c)

d)

Or in rhythmical figures:

Or:– B, For smaller hands

[Also other figurations as in set. Ⓐ]

Or on these notes—a slightly
larger extension.

etc.

Those who feel they would like to contract the hand after these severe extensions, will find the first set of Full contraction exercises, Section V, useful.

SECOND DAILY EXERCISE

FOR HORIZONTAL FREEDOM
(of Thumb, Hand, and Forearm) and for Agility COMPULSION.

Directions :

This should be practised *Prestissimo* ; since the quicker it is played, the more is one *compelled* not to linger on the keybeds. Repetitions of the same note *at speed* actually do not admit of this fault, hence the great utility of this exercise towards accomplishing the trick of Agility, which depends mostly on accuracy in timing the *cessation* of each key-impulse the instant its mission is completed. See to it therefore that the keys are here again allowed to bounce back. The arm must be " light ", as for all Agility, so that the repetitions can be played cleanly.

It is imperative to insist on freedom in the side-to-side movements of the thumb and hand. Be sure, when the thumb is swung round to meet the fifth finger note, that the hand freely swings outwards at the wrist joint. This essential is likely to escape you, if not carefully attended to throughout the exercise.

The elbows themselves should remain quiescent—held slightly outwards—this also is most essential.

Above all, insist upon Freedom—freedom in the action of poising the arm, freedom in the horizontal movements, and freedom in the exertions of the finger and hand in making the tones, which mean elision of all contrary (or antagonistic) exertions. Only bad players play more stiffly the quicker and faster they play !

This may also be practised in similar motion between the two hands, viz:—

etc.

In place of the thrice repeated notes, now give six repetitions each time, thus:

Prestissimo

etc, etc.

This is the best form of this exercise, and is extraordinarily effective for promoting agility. Often practice **pp** while insisting on Eveness.

An alternative Exercise:—

Lightly

8

Or by similar motion:—

etc. etc.

Or these:—

Or on:—

On to

and so on

Maj. 5/3   Min. 5/3   Min. 6/3   Maj. 6/3   Maj. 6/4   Min. 6/4

Or this form of it:—

Or:—

Variante of the Second Exercise :

This alternative variation is even more searching for horizontal (or lateral) freedom, than the original exercise. It is well to wind up the practice of No. 2 with this " close-up " form of it.

Be most careful, as in the first version, to give the fullest possible side-to-side movement of the wrist, swinging it well outwards when the thumb goes under, but nevertheless *without* any movement of the Elbow.

VARIANTE:

a)

Or accent it: *etc.*

b)

Or accent it: *etc.*

Also: Practise other keys; or chromatic scale.

Four Daily Exercises

THIRD DAILY EXERCISE
REPETITION ON DOUBLE NOTES
(Exercise to induce Agility – power)

Directions :

This Double Thirds *five finger exercise on repeated notes* I find to be a most searching one for " finger-individualization " and Agility. It may sometimes be played by actual Hand-movement (so-called " wrist-touch ") but its main practice should be by *finger-movement* only (" finger-touch ").

Be careful : (1) To Keep Elbow and Wrist quiet.

(2) To allow the hand to be quite FREE in its necessary side-to-side movements to bring the successive fingers over their keys.

Occasionally play it " *forte*," but most of the practice should be " *p* ", and even " *pp* ". In fact the best form of practice here is " *pp* " produced by only the " small muscles of the fingers " (see page 43 " The Visible and Invisible "), played *legatissimo* all through, and perfectly evenly.

While notes cannot possibly be repeated rapidly unless the keys are allowed to *rebound* from the key-beds (as in all Agility exercises), yet this rebound may be " caught " at key-surface by the next two fingers ; or, what is better still, by making the exchange of fingers *with the keys remaining half-way down*. This is difficult, but forms splendid discipline. In fact you are then playing both staccato and legato at the same time—staccatissimo at the bottom of the key and yet legato *midway down* !

This exercise, like the last one, is designed as practice for, and as an agent towards Agility. It is almost impossible to practise such rapid reiterations without unconsciously provoking the acquisition of Agility itself. This, as all along insisted upon, mainly depends upon strict obedience to the two main mental, physical and physiological conditions concerned. Thus let me repeat it, (1) accuracy in timing the propulsion of each key " to sound " only, thus avoiding its being jammed down upon the keybeds ; and (2) the poised arm-condition which renders this possible. Hence, for Agility, the tone-producing process can never take longer than in strictest *staccatissimo*. Instantaneous *key-rebound* ensures this.

This exercise should therefore again be practised as swiftly as possible, so as to compel such rebounding key.

At times, instead of Finger-movement, it may instead be practised by Hand movement (so-called " Wrist-touch ") ; finger-movement, however, should usually be employed, and even this without more actual movement than absolutely essential—in fact at such times you may start from key-surface—or even half-way down. It is good, sometimes, to practise quite softly, and combining staccato *tone-production* with *legato* effect !

This can be accomplished by insisting (as before explained) upon the rebound of the key off its bed, but not allowing it to rise more than about half-way up or so. In this case the dampers fail to reach the strings, and thus the effect is a true legato, in spite of the partial key-rebound.

In this exercise the successive fingers are brought over their respective notes solely by free horizontal (lateral) movements of the hand and the wrist-joint, while the elbow remains quiescent. The hand also remains lying loosely on the key-board. The forearm, rotarily, must be left unimpeded ; the weak, small, rotatory muscles here amply serve to keep the hand in its horizontal position.

Sometimes practise *forte*, but mostly quite *piano* since any deviation from evenness is then more easily noticeable.

May also be practised in rhythmical figures:—

etc.

This SILENT EXERCISE for legato is also useful at times, and may be practised on a table at odd moments. It is rather an experimental than every-day exercise.

Keep fingers at bottom level of Keys— or table— and substitute new fingers without any break of continuity, the new fingers sliding over or under the previous ones.

It is even useful sometimes to play the exercise on single notes. Thus:—

Presto

Or:—

Or better still, with *double-notes fingering*, on single notes; Thus:—

Or:—

Or:— 3   5   2   4   1   3   2   4

FOURTH DAILY EXERCISE

CLOSEST POSITION ARPEGGIO
and
"Kick-off" and "Float-off" practice
—again for the attainment of true Agility

Directions for No. 4—Closest position Arpeggio:

It is always well to wind-up ones daily preparatory technical practice with a few of these arpeggios. Also, they admirably serve us to become used to a new keyboard.

They prompt towards the acquisition and retention of Agility, since played at speed the hand that travels first *must* be played *staccatissimo*, else the following hand cannot sound its notes. The arm, therefore, as in all Agility playing, must be light.

It can be played either (1) in the "kick-off" form, or (2) in the "float-off" form. In the first form the thumb (or fifth finger) gives an accent on the last note of the arpeggio, and it should feel as if the arm were sprung up into the air by this impact; but in the second form (without such accent) the arm should gently float up from the keyboard.

In both forms it is the rising key of the last note that should prompt and time the "up" muscles of the arm into action.

It is useful to practise (either form) (1), with the whole arm from the shoulder thus rising, or (2), with the Forearm (from the Elbow) alone thus rising. This raising of the arm at the end of the arpeggio prompts one to keep the arm "off" also during the preceding rush of notes, and thus helps towards the acquisition of that trick of the "poised arm"—so essential in all Agility playing.

This exercise is given (by permission of Messrs. Bosworth) from my "Relaxation Studies", where a whole chapter is devoted to its elucidation—p. 81.

H. 15119

Or:—on a semitone higher—[a] to [f]

Four Daily Exercises

H. 15119

14

and same chords as before:-

Or again on a
note higher:—

Or on these:—

| Major | Minor | Major | Minor | Major | Minor |

Or:—

etc.

Or this closest position arpeggio as one figuration up and down. Or taken bending back on itself, thus:-

etc.

SOME EXTRA TECHNIQUES

No.1. ON FULLEST CONTRACTION

Fullest Contraction Five-finger Exercises:-

d Or with reversed accents. Or with *l.h.* my similar motion:—

etc. Or on other notes.

f also actually on same note, Thus:-

Presto

g Or in triples instead:

H. 15119

Or in still closer, and closest contractions, as already noted on page 14 under double-note repetitions.

Turn wrist outwards, (or hand inwards) Insist on horizontal freedom of the hand, and remain close to Keys:—

No. 2. SUSTAINED NOTES EXERCISES

Directions :

We all suffered in our youth from the infliction of this exercise. As then taught nothing could have been better calculated to prevent our ever attaining a free, easy Technique ! Our teachers used to tell us to hold the sustained notes down " firmly " —the more firmly and forcibly the notes were held the more helpful was it supposed to be ! and it certainly proved an effective obstacle to Pianistic progress, and oftentimes caused wrecked hands.

Taught correctly, however, this very exercise can prove to be extraordinarily effective towards Finger-individualization. But you must *not* hold the notes down " firmly " —on the contrary they must be kept depressed as lightly as possible. In fact at the beginning this exercise can at once show the distinction between the perhaps strong action of sounding the notes, and the always light action of holding them down—a changing over from the " strong " finger muscles to the weak ones. I have in most of my books quoted the best form of this exercise for this purpose. For instance :

. Sound strongly and at once hold lightly. Sustain the holding note so lightly that the knuckles of the hand remain quite movable (vertically) while sounding the other two notes.

The following may be practised on a table at odd moments, bent or flat fingers— quite good for concentration!

Or instead of **A**, the following simpler form:-

Or these more difficult forms:-

Always remember: After sounding strongly, hold lightly.

Four Daily Exercises

The exercises which follow are to be taken more as a *jeu d'esprit* than as serious study. Advanced players, however, will find them entertaining at times, and even quite useful !

✱ *Held, but not sounded*

etc.

Extra Exercise No.3

For Horizontal (or lateral) Freedom of Thumb, Fingers, Hand and Wrist.

This now almost ancient exercise of mine still remains invaluable for its purpose, and can often be of use even to the most advanced player, hence its inclusion here. Insist upon perfect freedom in the movements, and practise it for the most part with a perfectly resilient key:— *i.e.* with correct "agility touch."

a **For fingers over thumb:**

also:-
```
1.3.1.3.
1.4.1.4.
1.5.1.5.
```

b **For thumb under fingers:**

also:-
```
1.3.1.3.
1.4.1.4.
1.5.1.5.
```

H. 15119

Extra Exercise No. 4.
FOR "LIGHTNING" OCTAVES

Directions for Extra Exercise. No. 4.

I have been asked to give an exercise for this. The only possible answer is, that Agility in octave playing depends precisely on the same elements as all other Agility. In the first place it demands absolute accuracy in the "aiming" of each tone-producing impulse, so that the hand may be instantly free to engage the next two keys. In "Relaxation Studies" I have given a full description of the several steps implied in learning to play octaves; and how to apply the Forearm-rotatory element for each octave freely and individually. The most important exercise towards speed in octave progression is also there quoted; and I append that exercise herewith.. You here sound each octave with perfectly rebounding keys and allow these rising keys as it were to bounce you on to the next octave, but without sounding this next octave. Be careful to avoid giving two impulses, instead allow the rising first octave to prompt the instantaneous movement horizontally to the next one. After that you then sound this, and again let it carry you instantaneously to the next one. After having repeated this series of sharp movements from note to note—a *glissando* movement at the surface of the keyboard—quite a number of times up the given arpeggio, then take the whole arpeggio *as one continuous slide*, sounding all the octaves as you pass over them, practically by finger action alone; the "small" rotary muscles of the forearm here keep the hand in its level position in the meantime. It is to be noted that *Theodor Leschetizki* invented this very same exercise—we did so quite independently of each other! This forms good proof of its having being conceived logically by both of us, and this forms a strong recommendation for its practice.

The final result is analogous to a glissando along the keyboard surface, and yet with light soundings of each octave, solely by *finger-movement*.

The long note is not to be sounded, but to be reached instantaneously and silently, and as a rebound from the preceding note. Insist on this being one action and not two.

Also on other chords and on longer arpeggios at times.

Note:— From Chapter XV, and page 36 "Relaxation Studies" (by permission of Messrs. Bosworth & Cᵒ) which see.

Extra Exercise No. 5.
Interspersed double-notes. (mainly a mental exercise!)

Or:—

C

Or:—

Also start with *l.h.*
instead of *r.h.*

No. 6.
CHOPIN STUDY

Directions:

In practising this *Chopin* Study, either in the original or in this more difficult version, the most important point to attend to is the way these extreme extension groups are joined up.

In this present study, in ascending, the thumb has to be brought close up to the fifth finger each time, and this should be accomplished not by turning the wrist outwards each time, but instead by letting the fifth finger as it were double-over upon itself, its nail-joint turning under. Thus in giving way, it allows the thumb (with the forearm) to creep up. The wrist, if anything, here turns inwards during the process. In descending, it is the nail-joint of the thumb that must give way each time, and curl inwards after sounding its note, and it thus allows the fifth finger to reach its note, the hand turning inwards in the meantime. (** Next page.*)

Practise Chopin's Study in C. Op. 10, N° 1 thus, and all through:—

H. 15119

*I only quote the first phrase here ; later on, I hope to issue the whole study and several others. Such should certainly form the advanced student's and artist's " Daily Bread " in keeping his Technique up to the mark, and besides they form. musically, a quite inevitable part of his repertory.

Finally:- No.7.
THE OLD TWO-FINGER, RISING AND FALLING EXERCISE

The old *two-finger exercises* (rising and falling) are not to be despised, and may often be practised with advantage. FRANZ LISZT, in his old days, seems to have had great faith in them, and practised them himself. Provided they are practised with light arm and loose-lying hand, and with perfect freedom and accuracy in " aiming " each tone, they serve well to " keep one's fingers in". Here are a few versions :—

And with accents reversed

Or taken on any other scale— same fingerings.

Or on chromatic scale— same fingerings

Or reversed accents

H. 15119

Or in double notes

Or with accents reversed
etc. and all keys (same
fingerings)

d)

Or chromatically

And with accentuation
etc. reversed.

Be sure to play *lightly:-* arm "off" with hand lying loosely on the keyboard. Play accurately "to the sound," so that keys remain resilient. Practise at good speed. Do not strum, but always play musically— and therefore not too long at a time.

The Purpose of Technical Exercises.

Some 35 years ago, in my first book " The Act of Touch," I promised to issue a collection of " Occasional Technics "; this, however, has been delayed till now. The purpose of " Technics " in days past was quite a different one to what it is now. In the old days, since no one knew anything of the simple fundamental facts of piano technique, visible or invisible, all that the teacher could do, was to devise technical exercises that covered the ground. The hapless pupil then had to spend countless hours, months and years in the (supposed) practice of these exercises with the faint hope that by experimental failure, or by rare, occasional lucky success, he might perchance discover for himself the sensations accompanying successful DOING. For the most part, of course, the result was miserable failure. Yet at that time it seemed the only possible way ever to acquire a technique such as the geniuses of the day did discover for themselves and proved in their playing.

All that is changed now, and to-day, we, teachers, can ensure that every pupil (even an intelligent child-beginner) can instantly be shown how to control good Tone, Duration and Agility. Yet, such fully-demonstrated and *right ways* of playing cannot become part of the player's equipment (his means of pianoforte-speech) until knowledge of the mechanical, physiological and even psychological facts has been turned into *automatic adjustments*, promptable by the sense of the music he wishes to express. To ensure such automatic, or semi-automatic response, the only way is often enough to repeat the correct processes. Endurance also has to be gained by this means. Much can and should here be done, by choosing actual music and musical studies which cover the ground. Obviously, to save time at this stage, some well chosen finger exercises should also here be used, but solely now-a-days for the opportunity of turning knowledge into physical habits, as before explained.

Moreover, Scales and Arpeggios must also be learnt in the early stages, for :

(1) promoting a strong sense of Tonality,
(2) developing a feeling for fundamental harmonies, and therefore also of their ornamentations, and finally for :
(3) a sense of fingering-positions.

The most advanced player also can derive benefit from a few exercises such as these " Four Exercises for Advanced Players and Artists".

Later on will also be issued " Occasional Technics " for less advanced students, and lastly a set for Beginners.

T. M.,
February, 1939

Educational Works for Pianoforte by
TOBIAS MATTHAY

THE ACT OF TOUCH.   With 22 Illustrations. 8vo, pp. xlii + 328.   10s. 6d.

'When Mr. Tobias Matthay first published his work, *The Act of Touch*, in 1903, it was received with very mixed feelings by the musical profession. Many scoffed at the mere fact that an acknowledged expert required some 300 pages of closely printed matter to explain how to play the pianoforte; others regarded the book as "a one-man's fad" which would have its day and be gone; others indignantly denied that anything could be wrong with existing methods, which had produced a Liszt, a Rubinstein, a Madame Schumann. But the wise, even if unable to grasp a tithe of the new gospel at first, recognized the fact that here was something giving food for thought and experiment.

'And now? The "one-man's fad" has within ten short years altered radically the whole system of modern pianoforte teaching. The Matthay Principles, Matthay Doctrines, Matthay Methods, call them what one may, are known the world over, and probably never before in art has an almost world-wide revolution been accomplished in so short a space of time. Truly of art did Schumann say, "Es ist des Lernens kein Ende".'—*Musical Times* (1913).

THE FIRST PRINCIPLES OF PIANOFORTE PLAYING. Being an extract from the Author's 'THE ACT OF TOUCH'. Designed for School use, and *with two additional chapters*—'Directions for Learners' and 'Advice to Teachers'. Crown 8vo.   4s. 6d.

COMMENTARIES ON THE TEACHING OF PIANOFORTE TECHNIQUE. A Supplement to 'THE ACT OF TOUCH' and 'FIRST PRINCIPLES'. Crown 8vo.   2s. 6d.
LONGMANS, GREEN & CO.

RELAXATION STUDIES. In the Muscular Discriminations required for Touch, Agility and Expression in Pianoforte Playing. Cloth bound (150 pages, 4to), with numerous Illustrations and Musical Examples; with a Portrait of the Author. 4to.   7s. 6d.
BOSWORTH & CO.

THE PRINCIPLES OF FINGERING, LAWS OF PEDALLING, &c. An Extract from above. 4to.
BOSWORTH & CO.   1s. 6d.

ON MEMORIZING and playing from memory and on Practice generally.   2s. net.

THE SLUR OR COUPLET of Notes in all its variety, its Interpretation and Execution. A Lecture: A Continuation of Musical Interpretation. With 96 Musical Examples.   4s. net.

THE ACT OF MUSICAL CONCENTRATION. A Lecture: The function of Analysis in playing. 2s. net.

THE VISIBLE AND INVISIBLE in Pianoforte Technique: A Summary of the Laws of Technique.   8s. 6d. net.

AN EPITOME from same (for School use).   3s. 6d. net.
OXFORD UNIVERSITY PRESS.

THE FOREARM ROTATION PRINCIPLE: ITS APPLICATION AND MASTERY. 4to, with Illustrations.   2s. 6d. net.
JOSEPH WILLIAMS, LTD.

THE CHILD'S FIRST STEPS IN PIANO PLAYING.§ Written for Children, but also for Adults as an Introduction to their teaching. 4to, with Illustrations.
JOSEPH WILLIAMS, LTD.   3s. net.

THE PIANIST'S FIRST MUSIC MAKING.§ The Music Material to accompany above, by FELIX SWINSTEAD and TOBIAS MATTHAY. (Anglo-French Series.) In Three Books. Books I and II, 3s.; Book III, 2s 6d.
OXFORD UNIVERSITY PRESS.

THE NINE STEPS TOWARDS FINGER INDIVIDUALIZATION.§ A supplement to 'THE PIANIST'S FIRST MUSIC MAKING' and 'THE CHILD'S FIRST STEPS'; and Summary of Technique. (Anglo-French Series.) 4to.   1s.
OXFORD UNIVERSITY PRESS.

These three together are in place of the now out-of-date 'Tutor.'

DOUBLE-THIRD SCALES: THEIR FINGERING AND PRACTICE. Practice Card No. 1   1s. 6d. net.
JOSEPH WILLIAMS, LTD.

MUSICAL INTERPRETATION. Its Laws and Principles, and their application in Teaching and Performing. Crown 8vo, with Illustrations, pp. xiv. + 163.   7s. 6d. net.
JOSEPH WILLIAMS, LTD.

THE T.M.P.S. PRACTICE TRIANGLE AND CARD. Exercises for Rotational Freedom, Finger Extension and Freeing. Triangle, 7s. 6d.; Card, 1s. 6d.
JOSEPH WILLIAMS, LTD.

THE PROBLEMS OF AGILITY. (Anglo-French Series.)   1s. 3d.
OXFORD UNIVERSITY PRESS.

ON METHOD IN TEACHING: A LECTURE. (Anglo-French Series.)   3s.

PIANO FALLACIES OF TO-DAY.   3s. 6d.

THREE PSYCHOLOGY LECTURES.   3s. 6d.
OXFORD UNIVERSITY PRESS.

FOUR DAILY EXERCISES, ETC., FOR ADVANCED STUDENTS AND ARTISTS. 3s. net.
BOOSEY & HAWKES, LTD.

Obtainable from
BOOSEY & HAWKES, LTD.
295 REGENT STREET, LONDON, W.1
NEW YORK: BOOSEY, HAWKES, BELWIN, INC.